PRENTICE HALL
SKILLS
INTERVENTION
KIT

Decimals

Randall I. Charles
Consultant
Professor Emeritus
Department of Mathematics and
Computer Science
San Jose State University
San Jose, California

Prentice
Hall

Glenview, Illinois
Needham, Massachusetts
Upper Saddle River, New Jersey

Staff Credits

Barbara Albright, Janet Fauser, Brian Kane, Marie Mathis, Sandra Morris, Cindy Noftle, Angie Seltzer, David B. Spangler, Jeff Weidenaar

Additional Credits

Steve Curtis Design, Inc., Barbara Hardt, Anne S. Ryan, Stet Graphics, Inc., Ziebka Editorial Services

ISBN: 0-13-043870-7

8 9 10 11 12 13 14   09 08 07 06 05

© Prentice-Hall, Inc.

Decimals

Table of Contents

SKILL 1: Reading and Writing Decimals

Each grid is separated into 100 sections of the same size, so each section represents one hundredth. The decimal shown is also written in a place-value chart, in number form, and in word form.

Place-value chart: ————————→

Number form: **1.29**

Word form: **one and twenty-nine hundredths**

Example 1

Write the decimal shown at the right in number form and in word form.

The grid is divided into 10 sections of the same size, so each section represents one tenth. Five sections are shaded.

Number form: 0.5   Word form: five tenths

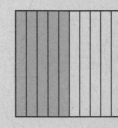

Example 2

Write *four and three hundred eleven thousandths* as a decimal.

The decimal point is read "and." A decimal in thousandths has three digits after the decimal point, so the decimal is 4.311.

Guided Practice

Write the decimal shown in number form and then in word form.

1. 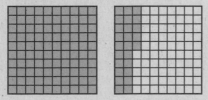   2.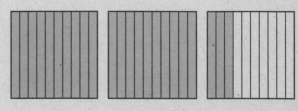

_____   _____

Write each number as a decimal.

3. eight hundredths _____   4. eight tenths _____

5. three and four hundred ninety-seven thousandths _____

Name _____ Date _____ Class _____

SKILL 1: Practice

Write each decimal shown in number form and in word form.

1.    **2.**    **3.**

_____   _____   _____

_____   _____   _____

Write each number as a decimal.

4. six hundredths _____   **5.** six tenths _____

6. six thousandths _____   **7.** fifteen ten-thousandths _____

8. fifty and four tenths _____   **9.** four and six hundredths _____

10. one hundred eight and ninety-five hundredths _____

11. two thousand four hundred seventy-five and one tenth _____

12. nine and four thousand one hundred twelve ten-thousandths _____

13. ninety-one and three hundred seven thousandths _____

14. nine hundred sixty-eight thousandths _____

Find each answer.

15. How many tenths are in 1 one? _____

16. How many hundredths are in 1 tenth? _____

17. Which decimal is shown below?

Skill 1

A 5.7   **C** 0.57

B 0.057   **D** 5700

18. Which decimal is read three and five hundredths?

Skill 1

F 0.35   **H** 3.005

G 3.05   **J** 3.50

Section A: Introduction to Decimals

SKILL 2: Equivalent Decimals and Writing a Decimal as a Fraction

Annexing, or writing, zeros to the right of the last nonzero digit in a decimal does not change the value of the decimal number.

Example 1

The same decimal is shown by each grid.

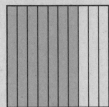 

0.7 and 0.70 are **equivalent** decimals.

0.7 = 0.70

0.7   0.70

Example 2

The grid at the right shows 67 hundredths. You can write this number as a decimal or as a fraction. Remember, a denominator of 100 shows hundredths.

$0.67 = \frac{67}{100}$

Guided Practice

Write each decimal as an equivalent decimal in hundredths.

1. 0.6 = 0.6_____   **2.** 5.9 = 5.9_____   **3.** 12.8 = _____   **4.** 0.200 = _____

Write each decimal as an equivalent decimal in thousandths.

5. 0.37 = 0.37____   **6.** 2.4 = 2.4_____   **7.** 6.05 = _____   **8.** 1.6 = _____

Write each decimal as a fraction or as a whole number and fraction.

9. $0.8 = \frac{\boxed{}}{10}$ **10.** $1.45 = 1\frac{\boxed{}}{100}$ **11.** $3.12 = 3\frac{\boxed{}}{\boxed{}}$ **12.** $0.167 = \frac{\boxed{}}{\boxed{}}$

Write each fraction as a decimal.

13. $\frac{42}{100} =$ _____   **14.** $\frac{371}{1,000} =$ _____   **15.** $1\frac{3}{10} =$ _____

16. $\frac{36}{1,000} =$ _____   **17.** $\frac{5}{100} =$ _____   **18.** $6\frac{1}{1,000} =$ _____

SKILL 2: Practice

Write a decimal and fraction for each number shown.

1.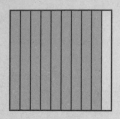

2.

3.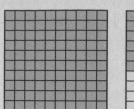

_____ = _____   _____ = _____   _____ = _____

Write each decimal as an equivalent decimal to the place value given.

4. 0.9 = _____ [thousandths]

5. 2.20 = _____ [tenths]

6. 1.25 = _____ [thousandths]

7. 9.8 = _____ [ten-thousandths]

8. 3.890 = _____ [hundredths]

9. 0.02 = _____ [thousandths]

10. 5.7 = _____ [hundredths]

11. 0.300 = _____ [tenths]

Write each decimal as a fraction or as a whole number and fraction.

12. 0.1 = _____   **13.** 1.5 = _____   **14.** 0.42 = _____   **15.** 0.2583 = _____

Write each fraction as a decimal.

16. $\frac{374}{1,000}$ = _____   **17.** $81\frac{7}{10}$ = _____   **18.** $1\frac{19}{100}$ = _____   **19.** $\frac{3}{100}$ = _____

There are 100 cents in a dollar, so writing dollars and cents is like writing a decimal in hundredths.

20. Write twelve dollars and fifty cents as a decimal.   _____

21. Write four dollars as a decimal.   _____

22. Write seventy-five cents as a decimal.   _____

23. Which is 1.4 written as a decimal in thousandths?

Skill 2

  A 1.400   **C** 1.40

  B 1.040   **D** 1.004

24. Which is the decimal for thirty-two hundredths?

Skill 1

  F 3200   **H** 32

  G 0.032   **J** 0.32

0.7 SKILL 3: Comparing and Ordering Decimals

To compare two decimals, write the decimals so that they have
the same number of digits after the decimal point. Then compare
the digit in each place value starting at the left.

Example 1

Use > or < to compare 0.08 and 0.6.

Step 1: Annex zeros so that both decimals have the same   0. 0 8
number of digits after the decimal point.   0. 6 **0**

Step 2: Compare the digits in each   The ones digits are the same.
place-value position, starting   Compare the digits
at the left.   in the tenths place. 6 > 0.

Since 6 tenths > 0 tenths, 0.6 > 0.08.

Example 2

Order from least to greatest: 0.725, 0.22, 1.7.

Annex zeros so all number are in thousandths.
Compare the ones. 1 > 0, so 1.7 is the greatest number.
Compare the tenths. 7 > 2, so 0.725 is the next number.
0.725 = 0.725   That means 0.22 must be the least number.
0.22 = 0.22**0**
1.7   = 1.7**00**   From least to greatest, the numbers are 0.22, 0.725, and 1.7.

Guided Practice

Use >, <, or = to compare 3.419 and 3.48.

1. a. Write 3.48 in thousandths. ———————

   b. Compare the digits. Start with the ones digit: 3 ◯ 3.

   Compare the tenths: 4 ◯ 4.

   Compare the hundredths: 1 ◯ 8.

   c. So, 3.419 ◯ 3.48.

Use >, <, or = to compare each pair of numbers.

2. 2.33 ◯ 2.033   **3.** 41.039 ◯ 41.05   **4.** 0.450 ◯ 0.45

Order from least to greatest.

5. 3.04, 0.304, 0.34   ———————————————

6. 11.011, 10.101, 10.011   ———————————————

SKILL 3: Practice

Use >, <, or = to compare each pair of numbers.

1. 0.4 ◯ 0.6   **2.** 2.46 ◯ 2.41   **3.** 9.83 ◯ 9.831

4. 0.5 ◯ 0.416   **5.** 0.387 ◯ 0.378   **6.** 4.8 ◯ 4.83

7. 12.75 ◯ 12.749   **8.** 5.03 ◯ 5.030   **9.** 23.65 ◯ 22.66

10. 7.382 ◯ 7.823   **11.** 89.6 ◯ 89.06   **12.** 5.36 ◯ 6.35

Order from least to greatest.

13. 0.4, 0.7, 0.3   **14.** 5.68, 5.73, 5.51

_____   _____

15. 21.6, 21.006, 21.06   **16.** 1.88, 0.888, 1.8

_____   _____

17. 8.23, 8.132, 8.123, 8.213   **18.** 6.57, 5.68, 5.67, 5.87

_____   _____

Find each answer.

19. Order the names of the cities shown in the table from the city with the greatest amount of rainfall to the city with the least amount of rainfall.

Rainfall (recent year)	
City	**Rainfall**
Atlanta	1.172 m
New York	1.237 m
Seattle	1.119 m

_____

20. Indianapolis had 1.193 meters of rainfall. After which city in your list would you put Indianapolis?

_____

21. Which list shows numbers in order from least to greatest?

Skill 3

A 2.3, 2.03, 2.033
B 2.03, 2.033, 2.3
C 2.3, 2.033, 2.03
D 2.033, 2.3, 2.03

22. Which is 1.042 written in words?

Skill 1

F one and forty-two hundredths
G one forty-two thousandths
H one and forty-two thousandths
J one thousand forty-two

0.7 **SKILL 4**: Rounding Decimals

The rules for rounding decimals are similar to those for rounding whole numbers.

Example 1

Round 34.0692 to the nearest hundredth.

Step 1: Find the place to which you want to round.

Step 2: Look at the digit to its right.

Step 3: If this digit is 5 or greater, round up. If it is less than 5, round down.

Step 4: Drop the digits to the right.

34.0692 — 6 is in the hundredths place.

— 9 is to the right of 6 hundredths. 9 > 5, so round up by adding 1 to the 6 and dropping the remaining digits to the right.

34.07 Round up to 34 and 7 hundredths.

So, 34.0692 rounded to the nearest hundredth is 34.07.

Example 2

Round 3.97 to the nearest tenth.

3.97 The digit to the right of 9 tenths is 7, so round up.

4.0 The 0 in the tenths place shows rounding to the nearest tenth.

3.97 rounds to 4.0 when rounded to the nearest tenth.

Example 3

Round $6.35 to the nearest dollar.

$6.35 The whole number is 6. The digit to the right is less than 5, so round down by dropping the digits to the right of the 6.

$6.35 rounds to $6, or $6.00, when rounded to the nearest dollar.

Guided Practice

Round 0.249 to the nearest tenth.

1. The tenths digit is _____.

2. The digit to the right of the tenths digit is _____.

3. Do you round up or down? Why? _____

4. To the nearest tenth, 0.249 rounds to _____.

Name the place value of the underlined digit. Then round to this place.

5. 4.6̲52

6. 19.30̲4

7. 59.9̲

_____   _____   _____

_____   _____

Name _____ Date _____ Class _____

SKILL 4: Practice

Give the place value of the underlined digit. Then round the number to this place value.

1. 42.4

_____

_____

2. 7.7961

_____

_____

3. 96.08

_____

_____

4. 1.881

_____

_____

5. 20.993

_____

_____

6. 13.2043

_____

_____

Round to the underlined place value.

7. 27.27

_____

8. 191.85

_____

9. 796.301

_____

10. 7.094

_____

11. 298.99

_____

12. 0.555

_____

13. 0.6921

_____

14. 409.7

_____

15. 0.607

_____

16. 1.009

_____

17. 33.255

_____

18. 1.02479

_____

19. 3.042

_____

20. 8.1919

_____

21. 50.96

_____

22. 71.6

_____

Marc said that to the nearest dollar, he spent $15.00 on a CD. Find each answer.

23. What is the least amount that Marc could have spent?

_____

24. What is the greatest amount that Marc could have spent?

_____

25. Which shows 1.356 rounded to the nearest tenth?

Skill 4

A 1.3   C 1.35

B 1.4   D 1.36

26. Which is 0.06 written as a fraction?

Skill 2

F $\frac{6}{1,000}$ H $\frac{6}{100}$

G $\frac{6}{10}$ J $\frac{100}{6}$

0.7 SKILL 5: Estimating Sums and Differences

You can use what you know about rounding decimals to estimate sums and differences. Round each number to the same place. Then add or subtract.

Example

Estimate: $12.89 + $14.29. Round to the nearest dollar.

Round each number to the nearest dollar by looking at the digit to the right of the ones place. Then add.

$$\begin{array}{rcl} \$\,12.89 & \longrightarrow & \$\,13 \\ +\,14.29 & \longrightarrow & +\,14 \\ \hline & & \$\,27 \end{array}$$

The estimated sum is $27.

Guided Practice

Estimate each sum or difference by first rounding each number to the nearest whole number.

1. Estimate: $12.897 - 4.331$.

$12.897 \to$ ___ Round to the nearest whole number.

$- 4.331 \to -$ ___

___ Then subtract.

2. Estimate: $23.443 + 5.09 + 0.87$.

$23.443 \to$ ___ Round to the nearest whole number.

$5.09 \to$ ___

$+ 0.87 \to +$ ___

___ Then add.

3. $\begin{array}{r} \$23.78 \\ + 79.82 \\ \hline \end{array}$

4. $\begin{array}{r} 71.089 \\ + 11.78 \\ \hline \end{array}$

5. $\begin{array}{r} \$54.88 \\ - 23.40 \\ \hline \end{array}$

6. $\begin{array}{r} 188.36 \\ - 59.99 \\ \hline \end{array}$

7. $3.49 + $7.73 + $2.52

_____

8. $16.662 - 10.25$

_____

9. $5.85 - $1.05

_____

10. $6.75 + $.80 + $2.10

_____

11. $121.5 - 0.95$

_____

12. $15.8 + 16.05 + 3$

_____

SKILL 5: Practice

Estimate by first rounding to the nearest whole number.

1.　30.2
　　+ 15.5

2.　99.7
　　+ 60.22

3.　4.216
　　+ 8.19

4.　$ 59.11
　　+ 37.95

5.　19.5
　　− 0.68

6.　20.35
　　− 14.527

7.　48.32
　　− 6.1

8.　$ 62.29
　　− 9.75

9. 3.9 + 35.4 _____

10. 78.03 − 10.4 _____

11. 88.4 + 5.2 + 6.7 _____

12. 47.3 + 8.92 + 2.0 _____

13. $71.94 − $4.28 _____

14. $88.40 + $8.55 _____

15. 37.941 − 13.07 _____

16. $147.80 − $104.50 _____

17. 5.6 + 13.1 _____

18. 30.3 + 21.7 _____

19. 3.7 − 0.81 _____

20. $19.25 − $3.95 _____

21. 17.012 − 1.8 _____

22. 65.75 + 13.02 _____

23. 18.65 + 2.3 _____

24. 31.26 + 0.995 _____

25. $1.99 + $3.40 + $ 3.88 + $0.97 _____

Solve.

26. Estimate the cost of a ball and a bat. _____

27. Estimate the cost of shoes and a glove. _____

28. Kim paid for a ball with a $20 bill.
Estimate how much change she received. _____

Baseball Equipment	
Shoes	$29.75
Bat	$16.49
Ball	$8.89
Glove	$19.19

29. Estimate the sum: 12.346 + 6.9.

Skill 5

A 20　　　　　**C** 19

B 18　　　　　**D** 18.246

30. Which number is greater than 1.104?

Skill 3

F 1.014　　　**H** 1.144

G 1.044　　　**J** 0.444

Section A: Introduction to Decimals

SKILL 6: Adding Decimals

When you add decimals, first line up the decimal points and put the decimal point in the answer. Annex zeros, if necessary so each decimal has the same number of decimal places. Then add.

Example

Add: 1.4 + 1.63.

Line up the decimal points. Put the decimal point in the answer.

↓

$$\begin{array}{r} 1.4 \\ + 1.63 \\ \hline . \end{array}$$

Write 1.4 in hundredths. Then add, beginning with the hundredths.

$$\begin{array}{r} {}^1 \\ 1.4\mathbf{0} \\ + 1.63 \\ \hline 3.03 \end{array}$$

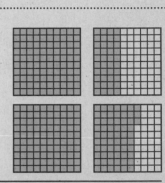

The sum of 1.4 and 1.63 is 3.03. The model shows this sum.

Guided Practice

Add.

1. 0.059 + 0.6

Line up the decimal points.
Put the decimal point in the answer.

↓

$$\begin{array}{r} 0.059 \\ + 0.6\mathbf{00} \\ \hline . \end{array}$$ Annex zeros to show thousandths. Then add.

2. 1.2 + 0.23 + 4

Line up the decimal points.
Put the decimal point in the answer.

↓

$$\begin{array}{r} 1.2\mathbf{0} \\ 0.23 \\ + 4.\mathbf{00} \\ \hline . \end{array}$$ Annex zeros to show hundredths. Then add.

3. 0.6 + 0.7

$\square$ Add the tenths.
0.6   6 tenths + 7 tenths = 13 tenths.
+ 0.7   Rename as 1 and 3 tenths.
$\square.\square$ Add the ones.

4. 3.05 + 2.09

$\square$
3.0 5
+ 2.0 9
$\square.\square\square$

5.
$$\begin{array}{r} 2.026 \\ + 0.42 \\ \hline \end{array}$$

6.
$$\begin{array}{r} 0.713 \\ + 3.8 \\ \hline \end{array}$$

7.
$$\begin{array}{r} 6 \\ + 8.21 \\ \hline \end{array}$$

8.
$$\begin{array}{r} 6.75 \\ + 15.33 \\ \hline \end{array}$$

9. 1.073 + 9.4 = _____

10. 14.72 + 27 + 0.629 = _____

SKILL 6: Practice

Add.

1. 0.6
    + 0.3

2. 0.9
    + 0.7

3. 2.9
    + 0.8

4. 1.08
    + 0.06

5. 6.4
    + 9.8

6. 82.07
    + 3.2

7. 8.37
    + 1.98

8. 1.02
    + 0.876

9. 42.9
    + 7.463

10. 1.806
     + 4.29

11. 10.8
     + 12

12. 13.8
     + 8.6

13. 75.452
     + 82.7

14. 13.06
     + 3.904

15. 6.256
     + 1.498

16. 43.007
     + 18.404

17. 0.5 + 0.5 = _____

18. 2.05 + 5.08 = _____

19. 50.5 + 8.176 = _____

20. 17.84 + 9.217 = _____

21. 0.6 + 9.75 + 11 = _____

22. 18.20 + 43.39 = _____

23. 0.25 + 4.086 = _____

24. 1.75 + 2.39 + 6.56 = _____

25. 8.91 + 11.4 + 0.006 = _____

26. 3.618 + 4.021 + 9 = _____

Solve.

The times for two teams in a 400-meter relay are shown in the table.

27. What was the total time for Team A? _____

28. What was the total time for Team B? _____

29. Which team won the relay? _____

400-Meter Relay		
Team	**lst 200 m**	**2nd 200 m**
Team A	2.92 min	4.01 min
Team B	3.00 min	3.95 min

TEST PREP

30. Add: 4.055 + 16.2.   *Skill 6*

    A 5.675   C 4.217
    B 20.255   D 10.255

31. Round 5.872 to the nearest tenth.   *Skill 4*

    F 5   H 5.8
    G 5.9   J 5.87

SKILL 7: Subtracting Decimals

When you subtract decimals, first line up the decimal points and put the decimal point in the answer. Annex zeros, if necessary, so each decimal has the same number of decimal places. Then subtract.

Example 1

Subtract: 30.07 − 4.9.

Line up the decimal points. Put the decimal point in the answer. Subtract the hundredths.	Since 9 > 0, you need to rename before you can subtract the tenths. Rename 3 tens as 2 tens and 10 ones.	Rename 10 ones as 9 ones and 10 tenths. Then finish subtracting, beginning with the tenths.

$$\begin{array}{r} 3\,0.0\,7 \\ -\;\;4.9\,0 \\ \hline .\;\;7 \end{array}$$

$$\begin{array}{r} {\scriptstyle 2\;10} \\ \cancel{3}\,\cancel{0}.0\,7 \\ -\;\;4.9\,0 \\ \hline .\;\;7 \end{array}$$

$$\begin{array}{r} {\scriptstyle \quad 9} \\ {\scriptstyle 2\;10\;10} \\ \cancel{3}\,\cancel{0}.\cancel{0}\,7 \\ -\;\;4.9\,0 \\ \hline 2\,5.1\,7 \end{array}$$

30.07 − 4.9 = 25.17.

Guided Practice

Subtract.

1. 1.006 − 0.8

Line up the decimal points.
Put the decimal point in the answer.
Annex zeros to show thousandths.

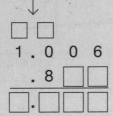

Subtract the thousandths and hundredths. When you subtract the tenths, first rename 1 one as 0 ones and 10 tenths.

2. 74 − 13.49

Line up the decimal points.
Put the decimal point in the answer.
Annex zeros to show hundredths.

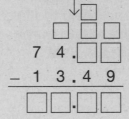

Before you subtract the hundredths, rename 4 ones as 3 ones and 10 tenths. Rename 10 tenths as 9 tenths and 10 hundredths. Then subtract.

3. $\begin{array}{r} 6.27 \\ -\,0.94 \\ \hline \end{array}$

4. $\begin{array}{r} 7.00 \\ -\,4.55 \\ \hline \end{array}$

5. $\begin{array}{r} 18.63 \\ -\,12.65 \\ \hline \end{array}$

6. $\begin{array}{r} 5 \\ -\,4.12 \\ \hline \end{array}$

7. 9 − 6.84 = _____

8. 50.87 − 4.271 = _____

9. 2.3 − 2.24 = _____

10. 10 − 1.1 = _____

SKILL 7: Practice

Subtract.

1. $\begin{array}{r} 9.8 \\ -7.8 \\ \hline \end{array}$

2. $\begin{array}{r} 47.09 \\ -36 \\ \hline \end{array}$

3. $\begin{array}{r} 8.25 \\ -6.62 \\ \hline \end{array}$

4. $\begin{array}{r} 65.42 \\ -41.6 \\ \hline \end{array}$

5. $\begin{array}{r} 3.421 \\ -0.409 \\ \hline \end{array}$

6. $\begin{array}{r} 9.3 \\ -4.546 \\ \hline \end{array}$

7. $\begin{array}{r} 62.04 \\ -29.004 \\ \hline \end{array}$

8. $\begin{array}{r} 18.902 \\ -6.604 \\ \hline \end{array}$

9. $\begin{array}{r} 15.306 \\ -8.73 \\ \hline \end{array}$

10. $\begin{array}{r} 14.3 \\ -3.429 \\ \hline \end{array}$

11. $\begin{array}{r} 63.48 \\ -53.7 \\ \hline \end{array}$

12. $\begin{array}{r} 37.49 \\ -33.922 \\ \hline \end{array}$

13. $16 - 15.86 =$ _____

14. $21 - 3.38 =$ _____

15. $91.96 - 90.97 =$ _____

16. $12.004 - 4.873 =$ _____

17. $49.071 - 20 =$ _____

18. $18.20 - 9.54 =$ _____

19. $74 - 15.473 =$ _____

20. $52 - 6.091 =$ _____

Solve.

21. You buy a CD for $12.99. You pay with a $20 bill. How much change should you get back? _____

22. The diagram shows the total length of the Mackinac Bridge, including the two approaches. What is the length of the main (middle) span of the bridge?

_____

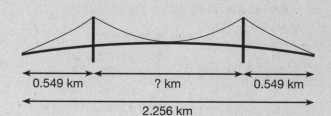

0.549 km   ? km   0.549 km

2.256 km

23. Subtract: $3.04 - 0.266$.

Skill 7

A 3.264   C 2.786

B 2.774   D 0.78

24. Estimate $13.455 + 59.845$. Round to the nearest whole number.

Skill 5

F 73   H 72

G 47   J 73.3

SKILL 8: PROBLEM SOLVING: Adding and Subtracting Decimals

When solving word problems involving addition or subtraction of decimals, it is important that you know when to add and when to subtract.

Example

The table shows that Fu Mingxia won the gold medal for platform diving in both 1992 and 1996. In 1996, she improved her score by 60.15 points. Find her 1996 score.

Olympic Platform Diving Gold Medal Winners		
Year	Diver	Points
1984	Zhou Jihong	435.51
1988	Xu Yanmel	445.20
1992	Fu Mingxia	461.43
1996	Fu Mingxia	

Read What are the key facts?

Plan Are you going to add or subtract?
Her score was 60.15 higher,
so add 461.43 and 60.15.

Solve Add.

$$
\begin{array}{rl}
461.43 & \leftarrow \ 1992\ \text{score} \\
+\ 60.15 & \leftarrow \ \text{Increase in score} \\
\hline
521.58 & \leftarrow \ 1996\ \text{score}
\end{array}
$$

Mingxia's 1996 score was 521.58 points.

Look Back See whether your answer makes sense.
Mingxia's 1996 score was higher than her 1992 score.
521.58 is greater than 461.43. The answer makes sense.

Guided Practice

**Compare Yanmel's 1988 score and Jihong's 1984 score.
How many more points did Yanmel score?**

1. How many points did Yanmel score? _____

2. How many points did Jihong score? _____

3. Will you add or subtract to find how
many more points Yanmel scored? _____

4. How many more points did Yanmel score? _____

**In springboard diving, Gao Min scored 580.23 points
in 1988 and 572.40 points in 1992.**

5. In which year did she score fewer points? _____

6. How many fewer points? _____

Name _____ Date _____ Class _____

SKILL 8: Practice

Solve each problem.

The table shows record catches for freshwater fish.

Record Fish Weights	
Largemouth Bass	22.25 lb
White Catfish	18.875 lb
Sockeye Salmon	15.1875 lb
Brook Trout	14.5 lb
Lake Whitefish	14.375 lb

1. What is the difference between the weight of the trout and the weight of the whitefish? _____

2. How much more did the bass weigh than the catfish? _____

3. Brian caught three brook trout that weighed 4.8 pounds, 3.54 pounds, and 2.71 pounds. What was the total weight of the three fish? _____

4. How much more did the record brook trout weigh than the three trout that Brian caught? _____

Use the map at the right.

5. How far is it from the tennis court to the beach by way of the ballpark? _____

6. How much shorter is the direct path from the tennis court to the beach than going to the beach by way of the ballpark? _____

7. How far is it around Sunset Park using the four outside paths? _____

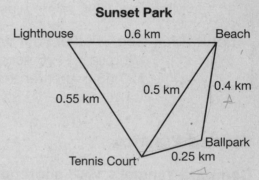

Sunset Park

Lighthouse — 0.6 km — Beach
0.55 km   0.5 km   0.4 km
Tennis Court — 0.25 km — Ballpark

TEST PREP

The odometer readings (in miles) on Mr. Quinlin's car are shown at the beginning of a trip and at the end of a trip.

Beginning:  1 2 3 0 2 . 9

End: 1 2 8 4 7 . 6

8. How far did he drive?

Skill 8

A 545.7 mi   C 544.7 mi
B 534.7 mi   D 5,150.5 mi

9. What is his ending reading rounded to the nearest whole mile?

Skill 4

F 12,847   H 12,850
G 12,848   J 12,847.6

0.7 **TEST PREP FOR SECTION A**

Circle each correct answer.

1. Which is 0.006 written as a fraction?

Skill 2

A $\frac{100}{6}$ **C** $\frac{6}{10}$

B $\frac{6}{1,000}$ **D** $\frac{6}{100}$

2. Which decimal is equivalent to 1.75?

Skill 2

F 1.075   **H** 1.705

G 0.175   **J** 1.750

3. Add: 4.7 + 3.54.

Skill 6

A 8.24   **C** 4.01

B 1.16   **D** 3.91

4. Subtract: 4 − 1.066.

Skill 7

F 2.934   **H** 3.944

G 5.066   **J** 2.944

5. Which is 8.95 rounded to the nearest whole number?

Skill 4

A 8   **C** 89

B 9   **D** 8.9

6. Estimate by rounding to the nearest whole number: 13.016 − 9.9.

Skill 5

F 3   **H** 4

G 22   **J** 14.116

7. Last spring Jamie planted a 2.8-foot tree. Since then it has grown 0.4 foot. How tall is the tree now?

Skill 8

A 2.4 feet   **C** 3.2 feet

B 2.2 feet   **D** 6.8 feet

8. Which decimal is less than 0.07?

Skill 3

F 0.077   **H** 0.007

G 0.7   **J** 0.77

9. Which list shows the numbers in order from greatest to least?

Skill 3

A 0.01, 0.101, 0.11

B 0.101, 0.11, 0.01

C 0.11, 0.101, 0.01

D 0.01, 0.11, 0.101

10. Write sixty-one hundredths as a decimal.

Skill 1

F 0.061   **H** 6100

G 610   **J** 0.61

11. Subtract: 4.6 − 0.08.

Skill 7

A 4.52   **C** 4.62

B 0.38   **D** 4.8

12. Estimate by first rounding to the nearest whole number: 43.56 + 21.4.

Skill 5

F 64.96   **H** 65

G 64   **J** 60

13. Which decimal is greater than 1.403?

Skill 3

A 1.41   **C** 1.4

B 1.403   **D** 1.04

14. Add: 6.675 + 0.4.

Skill 6

F 6.679   **H** 6.275

G 10.675   **J** 7.075

© Prentice-Hall, Inc.

0.7 Mixed Review for Section A

Why is a pencil like a riddle?

**To find out why, find the answer to each exercise at the bottom
of the page and write the letter on the blank above the answer.**

G   **1.**   Write eight tenths
as a decimal. _____

T   **2.**   Round 9.83 to the
nearest whole number. _____

W   **3.**   10.33 > _____. Which replaces
the blank: 10.3, 10.333, or 10.4?

N   **4.**   Write $4\frac{5}{10}$ as a decimal. _____

N   **5.**   Estimate 2.225 − 0.66. Round
to the nearest whole number. _____

O   **6.**   _____ < 1.06. Which replaces
the blank: 1.6, 1.066, or 1.006?

D   **7.**   Round 0.942 to
the nearest hundredth. _____

O   **8.**   0.34 + 1.26 = _____

T   **9.**   Write thirty-seven
hundredths as a decimal. _____

O   **10.**   Write $\frac{942}{1,000}$ as a decimal. _____

I   **11.**   Round 4.55 to
the nearest tenth. _____

T   **12.**   2.88 + 2.32 = _____

A   **13.**   16.45 + 4.05 = _____

U   **14.**   Estimate 36.87 − 17.4. Round
to the nearest whole number. _____

O   **15.**   _____ > 0.44. Which replaces
the blank: 0.4, 0.404, or 0.444?

H   **16.**   Write 0.080 in hundredths. _____

I   **17.**   Write $\frac{37}{1,000}$ as a decimal. _____

O   **18.**   Estimate 178.55 − 79.2. Round
to the nearest whole number. _____

P   **19.**   3.42 − 2.9 = _____

S   **20.**   6.3 + 3.12 = _____

I   **21.**   Write four and forty-four
hundredths as a decimal. _____

T   **22.**   6 − 3.995 = _____

———   ———   ———   ———   ———   ———   ———   ———   ———
4.6   2.005   9.42   4.5   1.6   0.8   0.942   100   0.94

———   ———   ———   ———   ———   ———   ———
10.3   0.037   10   0.08   0.444   20   0.37

———   ———   ———   ———   ———   ———
20.50   0.52   1.006   4.44   1   5.2

SKILL 9: Multiplying a Whole Number by a Decimal

One way to find the product of a decimal and a whole number, such as 3 × 0.45, is to use repeated addition. The grids show that 0.45 + 0.45 + 0.45 = 1.35.

To multiply a whole number by a decimal, multiply as you would whole numbers. Count the total number of digits to the right of the decimal point in both factors. Write the answer with the same number of decimal places.

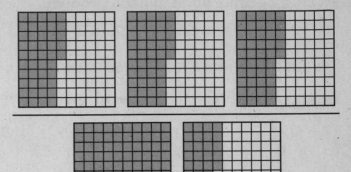

Example

Multiply: 3 × 0.45.

Count the digits to the right of the decimal point in each factor.

$$0.45 \leftarrow 2 \text{ decimal places}$$
$$\underline{\times\ 3} \leftarrow 0 \text{ decimal places}$$
$$\leftarrow 2 \text{ decimal places}$$

$$3 \times 0.45 = 1.35$$

Multiply.

$$45$$
$$\underline{\times\ 3}$$
$$135$$

Put the decimal point in the answer.

$$0.45$$
$$\underline{\times\ 3}$$
$$1.35$$

There are 2 digits after the decimal points in the factors, so the product has 2 decimal places.

Guided Practice

Place a decimal point in each product.

1. $1.279 \leftarrow 3$ decimal places
$\underline{\times\ \ \ 5} \leftarrow 0$ decimal places
$6395 \leftarrow$ _____ decimal places

2. $23 \leftarrow$ _____ decimal places
$\underline{\times\ 0.4} \leftarrow$ _____ decimal place
$92 \leftarrow$ _____ decimal place

3. $8.6 \leftarrow$ _____ decimal place
$\underline{\times\ 40} \leftarrow$ _____ decimal places
$3440 \leftarrow$ _____ decimal place

4. $49 \leftarrow$ _____ decimal places
$\underline{\times\ 0.016} \leftarrow$ _____ decimal places
294
$\underline{490}$
$784 \leftarrow$ _____ decimal places

Multiply.

5. $\$25.50 \times 7 =$ _____

6. $13 \times 0.274 =$ _____

SKILL 9: Practice

Place a decimal point in each product.

1. $12 \times 8.76 = 1\,0\,5\,1\,2$ **2.** $4.67 \times 7 = 3\,2\,6\,9$ **3.** $8 \times 17.6 = 1\,4\,0\,8$

4. $2.831 \times 3 = 8\,4\,9\,3$ **5.** $0.236 \times 21 = 4\,9\,5\,6$ **6.** $3.375 \times 8 = 2\,7\,0\,0\,0$

Multiply.

7. 0.4
  $\times\ 6$

8. 0.39
  $\times\ 3$

9. 0.12
  $\times\ 7$

10. 8.3
  $\times\ 6$

11. 0.208
  $\times\ 24$

12. 1.022
  $\times\ 15$

13. 3.7
  $\times\ 65$

14. 0.52
  $\times\ 26$

15. $324 \times 0.28 = $ _____

16. $\$25.98 \times 12 = $ _____

17. $1.65 \times 10 = $ _____

18. $8.111 \times 9 = $ _____

19. $18 \times 14.1 = $ _____

20. $6 \times 3.422 = $ _____

21. $\$1.02 \times 60 = $ _____

22. $9 \times 200.4 = $ _____

Solve.

23. The Beast, a roller coaster in Cincinnati, Ohio, is
1.4 miles long. How far would you travel in 5 rides? _____

24. The Dragon King in Salou, Spain, has a track that
is 0.789 mile long. How far would you travel in 3 rides? _____

TEST PREP

25. Multiply: 53×0.27.

Skill 9

A 4.77   **C** 1.431

B 14.31   **D** 143.1

26. Add: $4.86 + 3.7$.

Skill 6

F 7.56   **H** 8.5

G 8.56   **J** 4.33

SKILL 10: Multiplying a Decimal by 10, 100, or 1,000

Look for a pattern. Notice how the product increases and the decimal point moves when you multiply by 10, 100, or 1,000.

$10 \times 25 = 250$	$10 \times 2.5 = 25$	$10 \times 0.025 = 0.25$
$100 \times 25 = 2,500$	$100 \times 2.5 = 250$	$100 \times 0.025 = 2.5$
$1,000 \times 25 = 25,000$	$1,000 \times 2.5 = 2,500$	$1,000 \times 0.025 = 25$

To multiply by 10, 100, or 1,000, move the decimal point one place to the right for each zero in 10, 100, or 1,000. Sometimes you will need to annex zeros to show the product.

Example

Multiply 5.38 by 10, 100, and 1,000.

$5.38 \times 10 = 5\,3.8$ $5.38 \times 100 = 5\,38.$ $5.38 \times 1,000 = 5\,380.$

10 has one zero.   100 has two zeros.   1,000 has three zeros.
Move the decimal   Move the decimal   Move the decimal point
point one place   point two places   three places to the right.
to the right.   to the right.   Annex a zero.

$5.38 \times 10 = 53.8$ $5.38 \times 100 = 538$ $5.38 \times 1,000 = 5,380$

Note: When the product is a whole number, no decimal point is needed.

Guided Practice

Place the decimal point in the product. Annex zeros if necessary.

1. $3.185 \times 10 = 3\,1\,8\,5$ **2.** $3.185 \times 100 = 3\,1\,8\,5$ **3.** $3.185 \times 1,000 = 3\,1\,8\,5$

4. $7.84 \times 10 = 7\,8\,4$ **5.** $7.8 \times 100 = 7\,8$ **6.** $7.8 \times 1,000 = 7\,8$

7. $0.3 \times 10 = 0\,3$ **8.** $0.03 \times 100 = 0\,0\,3$ **9.** $0.03 \times 1,000 = 0\,0\,3$

Multiply.

10. $10 \times 0.6 =$ _____   **11.** $100 \times 0.043 =$ _____

12. $0.65 \times 1,000 =$ _____   **13.** $100 \times 0.007 =$ _____

14. $1.6537 \times 100 =$ _____   **15.** $0.0788 \times 1,000 =$ _____

Name _____ Date _____ Class _____

SKILL 10: Practice

Multiply.

1. $10 \times 0.5 =$ _____

2. $100 \times 0.05 =$ _____

3. $1{,}000 \times 0.005 =$ _____

4. $10 \times 0.67 =$ _____

5. $100 \times 0.67 =$ _____

6. $0.67 \times 1{,}000 =$ _____

7. $1{,}000 \times 3.42 =$ _____

8. $100 \times 45.6 =$ _____

9. $3.65 \times 1{,}000 =$ _____

10. $0.5713 \times 100 =$ _____

11. $0.008 \times 10 =$ _____

12. $8.9 \times 10 =$ _____

13. $10 \times 3.657 =$ _____

14. $0.06 \times 1{,}000 =$ _____

15. $1.12 \times 10 =$ _____

16. $0.4671 \times 1{,}000 =$ _____

17. $1{,}000 \times 0.001 \times 0 =$ _____

18. $100 \times 0.01 \times 100 =$ _____

19. $3.261 \times 1{,}000 =$ _____

20. $10 \times 0.004 =$ _____

21. $58.02 \times 100 =$ _____

22. $1{,}000 \times 7.2 =$ _____

23. $10 \times 0.389 =$ _____

24. $65.2 \times 1{,}000 =$ _____

Solve.

25. A baseball must weigh between 5 ounces and 5.25 ounces. Ten baseballs would weigh between

    _____ ounces and _____ ounces.

26. A tennis ball must weigh between 2 ounces and 2.065 ounces. Ten tennis balls would weigh

    between _____ ounces and _____ ounces.

27. A football must be at least 10.875 inches long. What is the shortest total length of 100 of these footballs laid end to end?   _____

28. Multiply: 26.7×100.

    Skill 10

    A 2,670   **C** 26,700

    B 0.267   **D** 267

29. Which number is less than 3.011?

    Skill 3

    F 3.111   **H** 3.001

    G 3.1   **J** 3.101

Section B: Multiplying Decimals

0.7

SKILL 11: Estimating Products

To estimate products, round each factor so that the computation is easy. Then multiply mentally.

Example 1

Estimate: 386 × 2.9.

386 × 2.9	Round 386 to 400.
↓ ↓	Round 2.9 to 3.
400 × 3 = 1,200	Multiply 400 × 3 mentally.

An estimate of this product is 1,200.

Example 2

Estimate: 0.75 × 6.099.

0.75 × 6.099	Round 0.75 to 0.8.
↓ ↓	Round 6.099 to 6.
0.8 × 6 = 4.8	Then multiply. Remember to put the decimal point in the answer.

An estimate of this product is 4.8.

Guided Practice

Estimate each product. Round each factor to make the computation easy.

1. 3.81 × 3.1
 ↓   ↓
 4 × 3 = _____

2. 12.34 × 9.5
  ↓   ↓
 10 × 10 = _____

3. 0.513 × 7.47
  ↓   ↓
 0.5 × 7 = _____

Estimate each product. Show what numbers you used.

4. 0.93 × 8.7
  ↓   ↓
 _____ × _____ = _____

5. 4.3 × 375.9
  ↓   ↓
 _____ × _____ = _____

6. 3.2 × 0.7
  ↓   ↓
 _____ × _____ = _____

7. 8.7 × 49.61
  ↓   ↓
 _____ × _____ = _____

8. 6.67 × 0.35
  ↓   ↓
 _____ × _____ = _____

9. 27.6 × 0.05
  ↓   ↓
 _____ × _____ = _____

SKILL 11: Practice

Estimate each product. Round to make the computation easy.

1. 6.43 × 8.7

↓ ↓

___ × ___ = _____

2. 34.5 × 9.6

↓ ↓

___ × ___ = _____

3. 3.07 × 1.85

↓ ↓

___ × ___ = _____

4. 93.9 × 0.4

↓ ↓

___ × ___ = _____

5. 0.49 × 5.1

↓ ↓

___ × ___ = _____

6. 106.9 × 0.008

↓ ↓

___ × ___ = _____

7. 9.832 × 6.5

_____

8. 14.3 × 7.08

_____

9. 22.049 × 3.27

_____

10. 4.63 × 0.9

_____

11. 6.2 × 7.746

_____

12. 317 × 0.4

_____

13. 6.15 × 99.9

_____

14. 0.609 × 21.4

_____

15. 7 × 0.083

_____

16. 0.9 × 7.9

_____

17. 32.1 × 4.8

_____

18. 105.2 × 3.8

_____

A light-year is the distance light travels in a year. It is about 9.5 trillion kilometers. Use this information to answer each question.

19. Alpha Centauri C is about 4.3 light-years from Earth. Estimate this distance in trillion kilometers. (Hint: Estimate 4.3 × 9.5.) _____

20. Sirius is about 8.6 light-years from Earth. Estimate this distance in trillion kilometers. _____

21. Which of these is the best estimate for 19.06 × 8.7?

Skill 11

A 180 **C** 1,800

B 18 **D** 0.018

22. Subtract: 9.7 − 0.74.

Skill 7

F 2.3 **H** 9.06

G 9.96 **J** 8.96

0.7

SKILL 12: Multiplying a Decimal by a Decimal

The rectangle on the grid is 0.8 unit long and 0.6 unit wide. Its area is 0.48 square unit, so 0.8 × 0.6 = 0.48.

To multiply two decimals, multiply as with whole numbers. Count the total number of digits to the right of the decimal point in both factors. Write the product with the same number of decimal places.

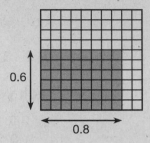

0.6

0.8

Example

Multiply: 0.48 × 0.52.

Count the digits top the right of the decimal point in each factor.

Multiply.

Put the decimal point in the answer.

```
  0.52  ← 2 decimal places          52              0.52
× 0.48  ← 2 decimal places        × 48            × 0.48
        ← 4 decimal places         416              416
                                   208              208
                                  2496             0.2496   Show 4 decimal places.
```

0.48 × 0.52 = 0.2496

Estimate to check your answer.

0.5 × 0.5 = 0.25. Since 0.25 is close to 0.2496, the answer is reasonable.

Guided Practice

Find each product. Check your answer by estimating.

1.
```
    16.6  ← _____ decimal place
  × 7.1   ← _____ decimal place
  □□□
□□□□
□□□□□  ← _____ decimal places
```
Estimate: _____ × _____ = _____

2.
```
    3.08  ← _____ decimal places
  × 8.9   ← _____ decimal place
□□□□□
□□□□
□□□□□  ← _____ decimal places
```
Estimate: _____ × _____ = _____

3. Multiply: 7.07 × 4.9.

   a. Total number of digits after the decimal point in the product: _____

   b. 707 × 49 = _____

   c. 7.07 × 4.9 = _____

   d. Estimated product: _____

Name _____ Date _____ Class _____

SKILL 12: Practice

Place a decimal point in each product.

1. $3.7 \times 19.8 = 7\ 3\ 2\ 6$ **2.** $5.7 \times 19.9 = 1\ 1\ 3\ 4\ 3$ **3.** $2.9 \times 13.82 = 4\ 0\ 0\ 7\ 8$

4. $10.2 \times 9.49 = 9\ 6\ 7\ 9\ 8$ **5.** $12.14 \times 8 = 9\ 7\ 1\ 2$ **6.** $0.02 \times 378.3 = 7\ 5\ 6\ 6$

Multiply. Estimate to check your answer.

7. 50.9
    $\times\ 0.9$

8. 0.91
    $\times\ 0.2$

9. 9.031
    $\times\ 0.5$

10. 0.36
    $\times\ 0.7$

11. 0.678
    $\times\ 1.2$

12. 9.2
    $\times\ 0.25$

13. 5.6
    $\times\ 4.8$

14. 12.52
    $\times\ 1.6$

15. $55.5 \times 0.7 =$ _____

16. $1.02 \times 0.6 =$ _____

17. $61.4 \times 0.5 =$ _____

18. $0.9 \times 200.4 =$ _____

19. $3.3 \times 38.8 =$ _____

20. $4.7 \times 8.12 =$ _____

**Solve. Remember that to find the area of a
rectangle, you multiply the length by the width.**

21. A rectangular park is 1.5 miles long and
1.2 miles wide. Find the area in square miles.   _____

22. A square floor tile measures 4.5 centimeters on
each side. Find the area of the tile in square centimeters.   _____

23. Multiply: 0.27×6.4.

Skill 12

 A 17.28   **C** 1.728
 B 572   **D** 1624

24. Pick a number so the decimals
are in order. 7.022, _____, 7.002.

Skill 3

 F 7.202   **H** 7.0
 G 7.22   **J** 7.02

© Prentice-Hall, Inc.

SKILL 13: Zeros in Decimal Products

When you multiply decimals, sometimes you must annex zeros
to have the correct number of digits to the right of the decimal point.

Example

Multiply: 0.31 × 0.18.

Count the numbers of digits
to the right of the decimal
point in each factor.   Multiply.

Annex zeros
as needed
in your answer.

$$\begin{array}{r} \textbf{0.18} \leftarrow 2 \text{ decimal places} \\ \underline{\times\, \textbf{0.31}} \leftarrow 2 \text{ decimal places} \\ \leftarrow 4 \text{ decimal places} \end{array}$$

$$\begin{array}{r} 18 \\ \underline{\times\, 31} \\ 18 \\ 54 \\ \hline 558 \end{array}$$

$$\begin{array}{r} 0.18 \\ \underline{\times\, 0.31} \\ 18 \\ 54 \\ \hline 0.0558 \end{array}$$

So, 0.31 × 0.18 = 0.0558.

Annex one zero so the
product has 4 decimal places.

Estimate to check your answer.
0.3 × 0.2 = 0.06.
Since 0.06 is close to 0.0558, the answer is reasonable.

Guided Practice

Find each product.

1.   0.1 0 2 ← _____ decimal places
    ×   0.4 5 ← _____ decimal places
    □□□
    □□□
    □□□□□□ ← _____ decimal places

2.   5.0 7 ← _____ decimal places
    × 0.0 0 7 3 ← _____ decimal places
    □□□□
    □□□□
    □□□□□□□ ← _____ decimal places

3. 0.0 2 8 ← _____ decimal places
    × 0.5 ← _____ decimal place
    ← _____ decimal places

4.   1.8 3 ← _____ decimal places
    × 0.0 4 ← _____ decimal places
    ← _____ decimal places

5. Multiply: 0.08 × 0.006.

   a. Total digits after the decimal point in the product: _____

   b. 8 × 6 = _____

   c. 0.08 × 0.006 = _____

SKILL 13: Practice

Find each product.

1. 0.028
  × 0.7

2. 1.83
  × 0.004

3. 0.0102
  × 0.045

4. 4.12
  × 0.0043

5. 2.3
  × 0.015

6. 0.17
  × 0.03

7. 0.45
  × 0.08

8. 0.098
  × 0.032

9. 0.035
  × 0.09

10. 2.34
  × 0.0005

11. 0.111
  × 0.04

12. 6.73
  × 0.011

13. $0.3 \times 0.002 =$ _____

14. $0.3 \times 0.2 =$ _____

15. $0.003 \times 0.02 =$ _____

16. $12 \times 0.0005 =$ _____

17. $0.09 \times 0.03 =$ _____

18. $0.07 \times 1.1 =$ _____

19. $0.003 \times 0.6 =$ _____

20. $1.003 \times 0.007 =$ _____

21. $0.67 \times 0.01 =$ _____

22. $2.3 \times 0.0003 =$ _____

Solve.

23. A pen costs $.75. Sales tax is 0.08 times the
cost of the pen. How much sales tax will be paid? _____

24. Find the product: 0.36×0.04.
  Skill 13

  A 0.0124   **C** 0.00124

  B 0.0144   **D** 0.00144

25. Find the difference: $3 - 0.02$.
  Skill 7

  F 0.01   **H** 2.98

  G 2.8   **J** 3.02

SKILL 14: PROBLEM SOLVING: Adding, Subtracting, and Multiplying Money

Computing with money is like computing with decimals.

Example

Kami bought 5 regular hamburgers. How much did the hamburgers cost?

Healthy Hamburgers Menu	
Regular Burger	$2.29
with cheese	$2.79
Deluxe Burger	$3.69
with cheese	$4.09
Salad	$1.59
Beverage	$1.10
Dessert	$1.39

Plan You are to find the total cost of 5 hamburgers. Since each hamburger costs the same amount, you can multiply.

Solve Multiply.

$ 2.29 ← Cost of one hamburger.
×   5 ← Kami bought 5 hamburgers.
$ 11.45 ← Total cost

The hamburgers cost $11.45.

Look back See if your answer makes sense. Each hamburger costs a little more than $2. Since 5 × $2 = $10, the answer makes sense.

Guided Practice

How much more does one deluxe hamburger cost than one regular hamburger?

1. How much does one deluxe hamburger cost? _____

2. How much does one regular hamburger cost? _____

3. How are you going to find how much more one deluxe hamburger costs? _____

4. How much more does one deluxe hamburger cost? _____

How much does a regular hamburger with cheese and a beverage cost?

5. How much does one hamburger with cheese cost? _____

6. How much does one beverage cost? _____

7. How are you going to find the answer? _____

8. How much does a regular hamburger with cheese and a beverage cost? _____

SKILL 14: Practice

Solve each problem.

1. Use the Healthy Hamburger Menu on the previous page. How much would a deluxe hamburger with cheese, a salad, and a beverage cost? _____

2. Lauren earns $4.50 an hour babysitting. How much will she earn in 3.5 hours? _____

3. How much change did Aaron get if he paid for a $6.25 movie ticket with a $20 bill? _____

4. Fines for overdue books at the Maple Park Library are $.08 a day. What is the fine for a book that has been overdue for 14 days? _____

5. Apples are on sale for $.85 a pound. How much would 2.5 pounds of apples cost? Round your answer to the nearest cent. _____

6. Ms. Ryder bought a birthday present for $18.75, a card for $1.98, and wrapping paper for $2. How much did she spend? _____

7. A CD was marked $12.50, but with sales tax it cost $13.56. How much was the sales tax? _____

8. Mr. Kenny bought 8.2 gallons of gasoline that cost $1.489 per gallon. How much did he pay for the gasoline? Round your answer to the nearest cent. _____

9. Randy has a coupon for $.50 off the rental of a video. How much would he pay for a video that rents for $2.49? _____

10. How much do you save by buying a 24-ounce box of corn flakes instead of two 12-ounce boxes?

    _____

$2.11
Corn Flakes
12 oz

$3.79
Corn Flakes
24 oz

TEST PREP

11. Frozen orange juice concentrate costs $.02 per ounce. How much does a 64-ounce container cost?

    Skill 14

    A $.13   **C** $12.80

    B $1.28   **D** $64.02

12. Which decimal is read two hundred twenty and four thousandths?

    Skill 1

    F 0.224   **H** 224,000

    G 220.04 **J** 220.004

0.7 TEST PREP FOR SECTION B

Circle each correct answer.

1. Estimate: 42.9 × 7.84.

Skill 11

A 32   **C** 3400
B 40   **D** 400

2. Multiply: 38 × 0.4.

Skill 9

F 152   **H** 15.2
G 1.52   **J** 12.2

3. Multiply: 9.2 × 0.5.

Skill 12

A 4.6   **C** 46
B 460   **D** 0.46

4. Multiply: 0.3 × 0.2.

Skill 13

F 0.06   **H** 6
G 0.006   **J** 0.6

5. Multiply: 13.6 × 0.8.

Skill 12

A 1.048   **C** 108.8
B 10.88   **D** 0.1088

6. Multiply: 1.7 × 0.03.

Skill 13

F 0.51   **H** 51,000
G 51   **J** 0.051

7. Multiply: 100 × 4.237.

Skill 10

A 0.04237   **C** 423.7
B 423,700   **D** 42.37

8. Multiply: 4 × 54.8.

Skill 9

F 219.2   **H** 2,192
G 2.192   **J** 21.92

9. Multiply: 6.4 × 6.4.

Skill 12

A 40.96   **C** 409.6
B 4.096   **D** 6.40

10. Shelly paid for a $7.59 paperback book with a $10 bill. How much change did she get back?

Skill 14

F $17.59   **H** $3
G $3.51   **J** $2.41

11. Multiply: 0.23 × 0.04.

Skill 13

A 82   **C** 0.0092
B 0.082   **D** 0.092

12. Estimate: 5.3 × 0.8.

Skill 11

F 0.40   **H** 40
G 4   **J** 48

13. The admission charge at the zoo is $3.75 per person. What is the total admission charge for a group of 28 people?

Skill 14

A $31.75   **C** $105.00
B $37.50   **D** $24.25

14. Multiply: 1,000 × 0.25.

Skill 10

F 0.00025   **H** 250
G 2,500   **J** 0.025

15. Multiply: 0.08 × 0.05.

Skill 13

A 0.4   **C** 40,000
B 0.004   **D** 0.4000

Mixed Review for Section B

Find each answer. Then shade the square that shows
the answer. A message will appear.

1. 0.54 × 29	**2.** 0.36 × 2.7	**3.** 0.3 × 0.2	**4.** 0.037 × 0.5
5. 0.51 × 7.2	**6.** 0.45 × 3.6	**7.** 0.13 × 0.65	**8.** 24.6 × 12

9. 100 × 2.8 = _____

10. 0.05 × 0.07 = _____

11. 59.4 × 10 = _____

12. 0.0678 × 100 = _____

13. 0.12 × 0.04 = _____

14. 1,000 × 0.7 = _____

15. 2.3 × 100 = _____

16. 10 × 8.4 = _____

17. 0.09 × 0.4 = _____

18. 0.3 × 0.09 = _____

19. 100 × 0.065 = _____

20. 0.0003 × 1,000 = _____

0.185	0.027	84.5	6.78	156.6	0.036	594	0.06	18.5
6	0.0845	59.4	84	367.2	28	1.62	67.8	0.65
0.162	0.0035	15.66	230	29.52	0.845	700	0.035	23
9.72	280	7,000	0.0048	0.006	0.84	3.672	0.048	16.2
36.72	295.2	0.0036	0.0185	3	6.5	0.972	0.3	0.27

Section B: Multiplying Decimals

SKILL 15: Dividing a Decimal by a Whole Number

The model shows that if you divide
1.8 into 3 equal parts, each part is 0.6.

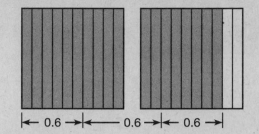

$$
\begin{array}{r}
0.6 \leftarrow \textbf{quotient} \\
3\overline{)1.8}
\end{array}
$$

divisor ↗   ↖ dividend

|← 0.6 →|← 0.6 →|← 0.6 →|

To divide a decimal by a whole number, first put the
decimal point in the quotient directly above the decimal
point in the dividend. Then divide as if you were dividing
whole numbers.

Example

Divide: 10.8 ÷ 4.

Put the decimal
point in the quotient.

$$4\overline{)10.8}\,{}^{.}$$

Divide 10 by 4. Write
the quotient above the 0.
Bring down the 8.

$$
\begin{array}{r}
2. \\
4\overline{)10.8} \\
8 \\
\hline
28
\end{array}
$$

Divide 28 by 4.

$$
\begin{array}{r}
2.7 \\
4\overline{)10.8} \\
8 \\
\hline
28 \\
28 \\
\hline
0
\end{array}
$$

10.8 ÷ 4 = 2.7

Guided Practice

**Find each quotient. Remember to put the decimal point in
the quotient.**

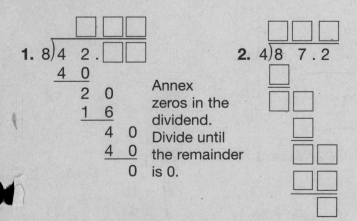

1. 8)4 2 .

$$
\begin{array}{r}
4\ 0 \\
\hline
2\ 0 \\
1\ 6 \\
\hline
4\ 0 \\
4\ 0 \\
\hline
0
\end{array}
$$

Annex
zeros in the
dividend.
Divide until
the remainder
is 0.

2. 4)8 7 . 2

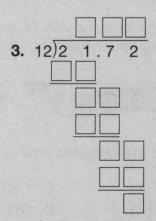

3. 12)2 1 . 7 2

Name _____   Date _____   Class _____

SKILL 15: Practice

Divide. Continue dividing until the remainder is 0.

1. $5\overline{)6.85}$ **2.** $3\overline{)13.68}$ **3.** $4\overline{)13}$ **4.** $8\overline{)52}$

5. $3\overline{)15.39}$ **6.** $6\overline{)404.4}$ **7.** $5\overline{)10.95}$ **8.** $6\overline{)28.5}$

9. $40\overline{)30}$ **10.** $15\overline{)61.65}$ **11.** $22\overline{)165}$ **12.** $65\overline{)240.5}$

13. $109.5 \div 75 =$ _____   **14.** $127.35 \div 45 =$ _____

15. $26.45 \div 23 =$ _____   **16.** $42.5 \div 25 =$ _____

17. $79.1 \div 14 =$ _____   **18.** $9.6417 \div 3 =$ _____

Solve.

19. A 5-pound beef roast costs $9.45.
What is the price per pound? _____

20. Sliced turkey costs $4 per pound. How
many pounds do you get for $16.20? _____

21. Find the quotient: $6.52 \div 4$.

                                Skill 15

    A 1.13   **C** 1.63

    B 16.3   **D** 163

22. Add: $0.73 + 4 + 2.8$.

                                  Skill 6

    F 6.53   **H** 1.05

    G 7.53   **J** 4.91

SKILL 16: Writing Zeros in the Quotient

Sometimes when you divide a decimal by a whole number, you have to write zeros in the quotient before you can start to divide.

Example

Divide: 1.475 ÷ 25.

Put the decimal point in the quotient.	There are no 25s in 1. Write 0 above the 1.	There are no 25s in 14. Write 0 above the 4.	Now divide.
$$25)\overline{1.475}$$	$$25)\overline{\overset{0.}{1.475}}$$	$$25)\overline{\overset{0.0}{1.475}}$$	$$\begin{array}{r} 0.059 \\ 25)\overline{1.475} \\ \underline{125} \\ 225 \\ \underline{225} \\ 0 \end{array}$$

1.475 ÷ 25 = 0.059

Guided Practice

Find each quotient.

1. $$\begin{array}{r} 0.\square\square \\ 5)\overline{0.45} \\ \underline{45} \\ 0 \end{array}$$

2. $$\begin{array}{r} 0.\square\square\square \\ 67)\overline{0.536} \\ \square\square \\ 0 \end{array}$$

3. $$\begin{array}{r} 0.\square\square\square \\ 92)\overline{0.368} \\ \square\square \\ \square \end{array}$$

4.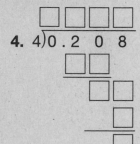

5.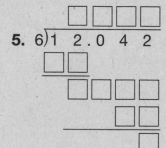

6.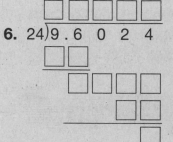

© Prentice-Hall, Inc.

SKILL 16: Practice

Find each quotient.

1. $4\overline{)0.28}$

2. $7\overline{)0.56}$

3. $2\overline{)6.018}$

4. $3\overline{)33.024}$

5. $6\overline{)0.096}$

6. $5\overline{)16.025}$

7. $24\overline{)72.48}$

8. $41\overline{)84.05}$

9. $65\overline{)2.405}$

10. $38\overline{)0.1558}$

11. $22\overline{)0.132}$

12. $25\overline{)2.15}$

13. $1.275 \div 75 =$ _____

14. $3.35 \div 50 =$ _____

15. $0.0135 \div 15 =$ _____

16. $18.585 \div 9 =$ _____

Solve.

17. A 10.5-inch sausage is cut into 150 slices of the same size. Is each slice greater than or less than 0.1 inch thick? _____

18. A stack of 250 sheets of bakery tissue paper is about 2.5 inches high. About how thick is each piece of tissue paper? _____

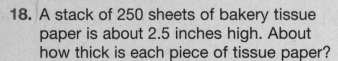

19. Divide: $0.054 \div 9$.

Skill 16

   A 0.6   **C** 0.006

   B 8   **D** 0.06

20. Multiply: 0.046×10.

Skill 10

   F 0.46   **H** 0.046

   G 4.6   **J** 460

0.7

SKILL 17: Dividing a Decimal by 10, 100, or 1,000

Notice how the quotient decreases and the decimal point moves
when you divide by 10, 100, or 1,000.

372 ÷ 10 = 37.2	6.2 ÷ 10 = 0.62	0.4 ÷ 10 = 0.04
372 ÷ 100 = 3.72	6.2 ÷ 100 = 0.062	0.4 ÷ 100 = 0.004
372 ÷ 1,000 = 0.372	6.2 ÷ 1,000 = 0.0062	0.4 ÷ 1,000 = 0.0004

To divide a number by 10, 100, or 1,000, move the decimal point one
place to the left for each zero in 10, 100, or 1,000. Sometimes you
will need to annex zeros to show the quotient.

Example

Divide 43.6 by 10, 100, and 1,000.

43.6 ÷ **10** = 4.36

10 has one zero.
Move the decimal
point one place
to the left.

43.6 ÷ 10 = 4.36

43.6 ÷ **100** = 0.436

100 has two zeros.
Move the decimal
point two places
to the left.

43.6 ÷ 100 = 0.436

43.6 ÷ **1,000** = 0.0436

1,000 has three zeros. Move
the decimal point three places
to the left. To do so, annex
a zero to the left of the 4.

43.6 ÷ 1,000 = 0.0436

Guided Practice

**Place the decimal point in the product.
Annex extra zeros if necessary.**

1. 48.1 ÷ 10 = 4 8 1   **2.** 48.1 ÷ 100 = 4 8 1   **3.** 48.1 ÷ 1,000 =   4 8 1

4. 278 ÷ 10 = 2 7 8   **5.** 278 ÷ 100 = 2 7 8   **6.** 278 ÷ 1,000 =   2 7 8

7. 0.9 ÷ 10 =   9   **8.** 0.9 ÷ 100 =   9   **9.** 0.9 ÷ 1,000 =   9

Divide.

10. 0.21 ÷ 10 = _____   **11.** 82.4 ÷ 1,000 = _____

12. 22.4 ÷ 100 = _____   **13.** 813.6 ÷ 10 = _____

14. 212 ÷ 1,000 = _____   **15.** 5 ÷ 100 = _____

16. 10 ÷ 1,000 = _____   **17.** 0.1 ÷ 1,000 = _____

SKILL 17: Practice

Divide.

1. 40.5 ÷ 100 = _____

2. 25 ÷ 1,000 = _____

3. 7.03 ÷ 100 = _____

4. 0.03 ÷ 10 = _____

5. 983 ÷ 100 = _____

6. 809 ÷ 1,000 = _____

7. 4,518 ÷ 100 = _____

8. 74.41 ÷ 10 = _____

9. 88.56 ÷ 10 = _____

10. 0.009 ÷ 10 = _____

11. 0.75 ÷ 100 = _____

12. 0.57 ÷ 100 = _____

13. 7.3 ÷ 1,000 = _____

14. 18,693 ÷ 100 = _____

15. 2.3 ÷ 100 = _____

16. 320.1 ÷ 1,000 = _____

17. 0.04 ÷ 100 = _____

18. 58.3 ÷ 1,000 = _____

19. 752.1 ÷ 10 = _____

20. 0.659 ÷ 100 = _____

21. 657 ÷ 10 = _____

22. 0.03 ÷ 1,000 = _____

23. 502.3 ÷ 100 = _____

24. 2,385 ÷ 1,000 = _____

25. 4.9 ÷ 10 = _____

26. 0.8 ÷ 100 = _____

Solve.

Mrs. Hanna paid a total of $59.00 for 10 identical
strands of lights to use for a party. The 10 strands
contained 1,000 lights in all.

27. How much did each strand of lights cost?   _____

28. How much did each light cost?   _____

29. Divide: 2.67 ÷ 100.

    Skill 17

  A 0.00267   C 0.0267

  B 0.267   D 267

30. Estimate: 3.95 × 46.8. Round to
make the computation easy.

    Skill 11

  F 200   H 250

  G 120   J 138

SKILL 18: PROBLEM SOLVING: Finding Averages

To find the average of a set of numbers, first find the sum
of the numbers. Then divide by the number of addends.

Example

The table shows the approximate duration of
the final 5 Apollo space missions. What was
the average duration of those missions?

APOLLO SPACE MISSIONS	
Apollo 13	6.0 days
Apollo 14	9.0 days
Apollo 15	12.3 days
Apollo 16	11.1 days
Apollo 17	12.6 days

Read The table shows the duration of the
final 5 Apollo missions.

Plan How do you find the average?
Add to find the total duration of the 5 missions.
Divide this sum by 5 to find the average.

Solve Add: 6.0 + 9.0 + 12.3 + 11.1 + 12.6 = 51.0.
Then divide.
The average duration of these missions was 10.2 days.

$$\begin{array}{r} 10.2 \\ 5\overline{)51.0} \\ \underline{5\,0} \\ 10 \\ \underline{10} \\ 0 \end{array}$$

Look Back The average should be between the least and
greatest addend. Since 10.2 is between 6.0 and
12.6, the answer makes sense.

Guided Practice

**Shawn's math test grades for the marking period
were 93, 85, 87, 67, 92, and 83. Find his average grade.**

1. What is the sum of the grades? _____

2. How many grades are there? _____

3. How do you find the average grade? _____

4. What is the average grade? _____

5. a. Is the average between the
least and greatest addend? _____

   b. Does the answer make sense? _____

6. Suppose Shawn's teacher throws out the
lowest test grade. Find Shawn's average
grade based on his five highest grades. _____

SKILL 18: Practice

Find the average of each set of numbers.

1. 1.6, 2.3, 2.3, 3.8, 2.0 _____

2. 0.33, 0.25, 0.26, 0.32 _____

Solve each problem.

3. The number of students in each homeroom at Lincoln School is 37, 41, 34, 38, 33, and 36. What is the average number of students in each room?

_____

4. The normal monthly precipitation in Baltimore, given in inches, is shown below.

3.1, 3.1, 3.4, 3.1, 3.7, 3.7,
3.7, 3.9, 3.4, 3.0, 3.3, 3.4

Find the average monthly precipitation.

_____

5. Shelly's times, in seconds, for the 100-meter dash were 21.2, 19.8, 22.1, 20.0, and 20.4. What is her average time?

_____

6. Larry bought CDs for $12.98, $15.39, and $8.95. What was the total amount he paid for the CDs?

_____

7. Ms. Kelstat bought milk four times last week. She paid the following for each gallon: $3.79, $3.53, $2.09 (on sale), $3.79. What was the average price per gallon?

$$\begin{array}{r} 1.2 \\ \times\ 4 \\ \hline 2|8 \end{array}$$

_____

8. Jamie took five tests and had an average score of 95.4. How many total points did she earn?

_____

9. Rosita's bowling scores were 129, 144, 137, and 148. Find her average score.

Skill 18

A 558   **C** 139.5

B 114   **D** 456

10. At 55 miles per hour, how far will Mr. Murray travel in 2.5 hours?

Skill 9

F 1,375 mi   **H** 57.5 mi

G 13.75 mi   **J** 137.5 mi

SKILL 19: Estimating Quotients

To estimate a quotient, choose numbers close to the
to the dividend and the divisor that are easy to divide.

Example 1

Estimate: 25.2 ÷ 6.4.

$$25.2 \div 6.4$$
$$\downarrow \qquad \downarrow$$
$$24 \div 6 = 4$$

Look at the divisor first. 6.4 is close to 6.
24 is a number close to 25.2 that is easy
to divide by 6.

An estimated quotient is 4.

Example 2

Estimate: 189.44 ÷ 26.
$$\downarrow \qquad \downarrow$$
$$200 \div 25 = 8$$

An estimated quotient is 8.

Guided Practice

Estimate each quotient.

1. 154.1 ÷ 46.9
$\downarrow \qquad \downarrow$
150 ÷ 50 = _____

2. 57.9 ÷ 8
$\downarrow \qquad \downarrow$
56 ÷ 8 = _____

3. 9.16 ÷ 5.2
$\downarrow \qquad \downarrow$
10 ÷ 5 = _____

Estimate each quotient. Show what numbers you used.

4. 35.9 ÷ 8.7
$\downarrow \qquad \downarrow$
_____ ÷ _____ = _____

5. 392.7 ÷ 4.2
$\downarrow \qquad \downarrow$
_____ ÷ _____ = _____

6. 23.8 ÷ 8
$\downarrow \qquad \downarrow$
_____ ÷ _____ = _____

7. 46.2 ÷ 9
$\downarrow \qquad \downarrow$
_____ ÷ _____ = _____

8. 486.1 ÷ 24.9
$\downarrow \qquad \downarrow$
_____ ÷ _____ = _____

9. 17.1 ÷ 3.2
$\downarrow \qquad \downarrow$
_____ ÷ _____ = _____

10. 53.1 ÷ 5.9
$\downarrow \qquad \downarrow$
_____ ÷ _____ = _____

11. 62 ÷ 9.8
$\downarrow \qquad \downarrow$
_____ ÷ _____ = _____

12. 50 ÷ 7.1
$\downarrow \qquad \downarrow$
_____ ÷ _____ = _____

© Prentice-Hall, Inc.

SKILL 19: Practice

Estimate each quotient.

1. 37.16 ÷ 8.7 _____

2. 121.7 ÷ 2.9 _____

3. 14.6 ÷ 6.8 _____

4. 80.1 ÷ 4 _____

5. 515.3 ÷ 56 _____

6. 106.9 ÷ 0.95 _____

7. 245.6 ÷ 59 _____

8. 16.42 ÷ 8 _____

9. 76.7 ÷ 25 _____

10. 271.3 ÷ 9.03 _____

11. 798.6 ÷ 38.5 _____

12. 42.8 ÷ 6.7 _____

13. 13.86 ÷ 2.3 _____

14. 62.1 ÷ 5.8 _____

15. 608.7 ÷ 19 _____

16. 36.1 ÷ 12.2 _____

Use estimation to solve.

17. Lynne bought 12 golf balls for $14.98. Did each
golf ball cost more than or less than $1.00?   _____

18. The track team paid $179.50 for 9 sweatshirts.
About how much did each sweatshirt cost?   _____

19. The soccer coach bought 5 packages of socks for $46.25.
Each package contained 3 pairs of socks. If he sells the
socks to his players for $3.00 a pair, will he lose money? Explain.

_____

20. Estimate: 34.6 ÷ 7.

Skill 19

   A 50   **C** 5

   B 0.5   **D** 4

21. Subtract: 19.7 − 1.74.

Skill 7

   F 0.23   **H** 2.3

   G 17.96   **J** 18.06

SKILL 20: Dividing a Whole Number by a Decimal

As illustrated below, you can multiply the dividend and divisor by the same nonzero number without changing the quotient.

$$6 \div 3 = \mathbf{2}$$ $$15 \div 5 = \mathbf{3}$$ $$0.46 \div 2 = \mathbf{0.23}$$
$$60 \div 30 = \mathbf{2}$$ $$1{,}500 \div 500 = \mathbf{3}$$ $$46 \div 200 = \mathbf{0.23}$$

    6 × 10   3 × 10   15 × 100   5 × 100   0.46 × 100   2 × 100

To divide by a decimal, multiply both the dividend and the divisor by 10, 100, or 1,000 so that the divisor is a whole number. Then put the decimal point in the quotient and divide.

Example

Divide: 63 ÷ 7.5.

Multiply the dividend and divisor by 10 so the divisor is a whole number.

$$7.5\overline{)63.0}$$

Put the decimal point in the quotient.

$$75\overline{)630.}\,\overset{\textstyle .}{}$$

Divide.

$$\begin{array}{r} 8.4 \\ 75\overline{)630.0} \\ \underline{600} \\ 300 \\ \underline{300} \\ 0 \end{array}$$

Annex a zero.
Divide until the remainder is zero.

$$63 \div 7.5 = 8.4$$

Guided Practice

Place the decimal point correctly in the quotient.

1. $0.6\overline{)12.0}$ 2 0

2. $0.5\overline{)66.0}$ 1 3 2

3. $2.5\overline{)16.00}$ 6 4

4. $0.48\overline{)36.00}$ 7 5

Divide.

5. $0.6\overline{)51}$

6. $0.4\overline{)7}$

7. $2.9\overline{)435}$

8. $0.15\overline{)126}$

SKILL 20: Practice

Divide.

1. $0.6\overline{)87}$

2. $0.06\overline{)87}$

3. $0.3\overline{)9}$

4. $0.03\overline{)9}$

5. $0.2\overline{)57}$

6. $0.8\overline{)10}$

7. $0.09\overline{)18}$

8. $0.04\overline{)13}$

9. $0.24\overline{)168}$

10. $1.2\overline{)15}$

11. $0.61\overline{)61}$

12. $0.35\overline{)98}$

13. $771 \div 0.12$ _____

14. $861 \div 8.4$ _____

15. $364 \div 0.56$ _____

16. $75 \div 0.025$ _____

Solve. Refer to the table.

17. How many $.33 stamps
can you buy for $33? _____

18. How many $.55 stamps
can you buy for $22? _____

Postal Rates for Letters	
1 ounce or less	$.33
Each additional ounce	$.22

19. **a.** What is the cost to mail a 3-ounce letter? _____

b. How many 3-ounce letters can you mail for $8? _____

20. Divide: $162 \div 2.7$.

Skill 20

A 600   **C** 6

B 0.6   **D** 60

21. Find the average: 6.7, 3, 8.6.

Skill 18

F 3   **H** 18.3

G 6.1   **J** 5.2

Section C: Dividing Decimals

0.7 *SKILL 21*: Dividing a Decimal by a Decimal

Remember that to divide by a decimal, multiply both the dividend and the divisor by 10, 100, or 1,000 so that the divisor is a whole number. Write the decimal point in the quotient and divide.

Example

Divide: 0.24 ÷ 3.2.

Multiply 3.2 and 0.24 by 10 so the divisor is a whole number.	Put the decimal point in the quotient.	There are no 32s in 2 or in 24. Write 0s in the quotient.	Annex zeros and continue dividing.
$3.2\overline{)0.24}$	$32\overline{)02.4}$	$32\overline{)02.4}$ (quotient 0.0)	$\begin{array}{r} 0.075 \\ 32\overline{)02.400} \\ \underline{2\,24} \\ 160 \\ \underline{160} \\ 0 \end{array}$

0.24 ÷ 3.2 = 0.075

Guided Practice

Place the decimal point correctly in each quotient.

1. $0.6\overline{)0.78}$ → 13

2. $0.25\overline{)4.25}$ → 17

3. $0.85\overline{)7.055}$ → 83

4. $3.7\overline{)1.036}$ → 028

5. $1.8\overline{)8.28}$ → 46

6. $0.63\overline{)0.6678}$ → 106

7. $0.04\overline{)0.916}$ → 229

8. $0.125\overline{)9.875}$ → 79

Divide.

9. $0.5\overline{)0.095}$

10. $0.9\overline{)1.08}$

11. $0.28\overline{)0.476}$

12. $0.7\overline{)0.0434}$

Name _____ Date _____ Class _____

SKILL 21: Practice

Divide.

1. $0.7\overline{)6.3}$ **2.** $0.9\overline{)0.18}$ **3.** $0.6\overline{)0.48}$ **4.** $0.8\overline{)1.12}$

5. $0.16\overline{)2.56}$ **6.** $0.36\overline{)0.288}$ **7.** $0.08\overline{)18}$ **8.** $1.4\overline{)13.86}$

9. $1.7\overline{)10.54}$ **10.** $2.4\overline{)0.168}$ **11.** $0.07\overline{)0.035}$ **12.** $0.96\overline{)0.0192}$

in out

13. $0.35 \div 0.07 =$ _____    **14.** $0.2068 \div 4.4 =$ _____

15. $0.015 \div 0.05 =$ _____   **16.** $13.76 \div 3.2 =$ _____

17. $0.441 \div 6.3 =$ _____   **18.** $0.0602 \div 0.086 =$ _____

Solve.

19. Teri paid $3.06 for apples that cost $.68 a pound. How many pounds of apples did she buy?   _____

20. Lin bought 9.2 gallons of gasoline for $12.42 and paid for it with a $20 bill. What was the price of one gallon of gasoline?   _____

21. Mr. Smith drove 381.9 miles in 8.5 hours. What was the average number of miles he drove each hour? Round your answer to the nearest tenth of a mile.   _____

TEST PREP

22. Divide: $0.288 \div 9.6$.

Skill 21

A 0.003   **C** 0.3

B 3   **D** 0.03

23. Find the product: 0.35×0.16.

Skill 13

F 0.056   **H** 0.56

G 0.530   **J** 5.60

0.7 TEST PREP FOR SECTION C

Circle each correct answer.

1. Estimate: 63.2 ÷ 8.7.

Skill 19

   A 70   **C** 7

   B 0.7   **D** 9

2. Divide: 51 ÷ 1.7.

Skill 20

   F 300   **H** 0.3

   G 30   **J** 3

3. Divide: 0.73 ÷ 10.

Skill 17

   A 0.073   **C** 7.3

   B 0.0073   **D** 0.73

4. Divide: 123.5 ÷ 5.

Skill 15

   F 24.7   **H** 20.1

   G 2.47   **J** 247

5. Divide: 21.7 ÷ 6.2.

Skill 21

   A 35   **C** 3.5

   B 3   **D** 0.35

6. Estimate: 153.9 ÷ 31.2.

Skill 19

   F 60   **H** 50

   G 5   **J** 0.5

7. Divide: 2.4 ÷ 32.

Skill 16

   A 7.5   **C** 0.0075

   B 0.075   **D** 0.75

8. Divide: 9.732 ÷ 3.

Skill 15

   F 32.44   **H** 3.214

   G 0.3244   **J** 3.244

9. Find the average of these grades: 82, 86, 74, and 92.

Skill 18

   A 334   **C** 86

   B 83.5   **D** 4

10. Divide: 0.04 ÷ 8.

Skill 16

   F 5   **H** 0.5

   G 0.05   **J** 0.005

11. Divide: 189 ÷ 7.5.

Skill 20

   A 252   **C** 2.52

   B 25.2   **D** 20.5

12. Divide: 0.072 ÷ 0.48.

Skill 21

   F 1.5   **H** 0.15

   G 15   **J** 1.7

13. Divide: 1.6 ÷ 1,000.

Skill 17

   A 0.16   **C** 16

   B 1600   **D** 0.0016

14. Find the average of 2.3, 2.8, and 3.

Skill 18

   F 2.7   **H** 8.1

   G 1.8   **J** 3

Mixed Review for Section C

Can you draw six straight lines through all the dots without lifting your pencil or retracing a line? To find the solution, first find each answer. Then trace through the dots in the order that the answers are given.

1. $14.8 \div 4 =$ _____

2. $3.3 \div 6 =$ _____

3. $47.6 \div 11.9 =$ _____

4. $35.1 \div 7.8 =$ _____

5. $15.96 \div 2.8 =$ _____

6. $8.829 \div 10 =$ _____

7. $165.6 \div 12 =$ _____

8. $840 \div 5.6 =$ _____

9. $0.6 \div 100 =$ _____

10. $0.795 \div 15 =$ _____

11. $0.629 \div 8.5 =$ _____

12. $49.74 \div 6 =$ _____

13. $39 \div 0.15 =$ _____

14. $228 \div 40 =$ _____

15. $0.172 \div 2 =$ _____

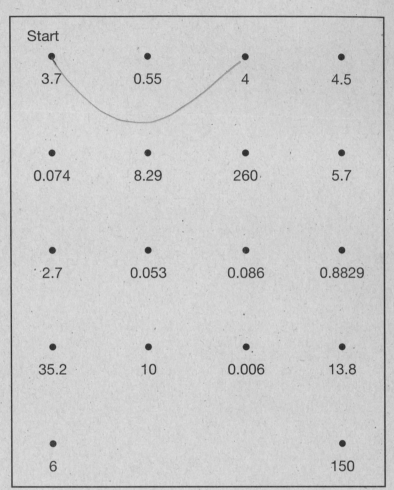

Start

3.7	0.55	4	4.5
0.074	8.29	260	5.7
2.7	0.053	0.086	0.8829
35.2	10	0.006	13.8
6			150

Estimate each quotient.

16. $126.7 \div 12.1$ _____

17. $43 \div 7.21$ _____

Find the average of each set of numbers.

18. 24.22 and 46.18 _____

19. 3.3, 4.9, 1.7, and 0.9 _____